Protecting Earth's Surface

Natalie Hyde

Crabtree Publishing Company
www.crabtreebooks.com

Author
Natalie Hyde

Publishing plan research and development
Reagan Miller

Editor
Crystal Sikkens

Proofreader and indexer
Wendy Scavuzzo

Design
Samara Parent

Photo research
Tammy McGarr

Prepress technician
Tammy McGarr

Print and production coordinator
Margaret Amy Salter

Photographs
Shutterstock: Title page © withGod; p5 © Richard Whitcombe;
    p7 © My Good Images; p10 © Imfoto; p18 © littleny
Thinkstock: p6 Stockbyte
Visuals Unlimited: p16 © Mark Gibson
Wikimedia Commons: p15 Robert Campbell; p17 Indolences

All other images from Shutterstock

Library and Archives Canada Cataloguing in Publication

Hyde, Natalie, 1963-, author
        Protecting Earth's surface / Natalie Hyde.

(Earth's processes close-up)
Includes index.
Issued in print and electronic formats.
ISBN 978-0-7787-1729-4 (bound).--ISBN 978-0-7787-1774-4 (paperback).--
ISBN 978-1-4271-1611-6 (pdf).--ISBN 978-1-4271-1607-9 (html)

        1. Environmental protection--Juvenile literature. 2. Environmental
engineering--Juvenile literature. I. Title.

TD170.15.H94 2015   j333.72   C2015-903929-0
                                             C2015-903930-4

Library of Congress Cataloging-in-Publication Data

CIP available at the Library of Congress

Crabtree Publishing Company

www.crabtreebooks.com   1-800-387-7650

Printed in Canada/102015/IH20150821

Published in Canada
Crabtree Publishing
616 Welland Ave.
St. Catharines, Ontario
L2M 5V6

Published in the United States
Crabtree Publishing
PMB 59051
350 Fifth Avenue, 59th Floor
New York, New York 10118

Published in the United Kingdom
Crabtree Publishing
Maritime House
Basin Road North, Hove
BN41 1WR

Published in Australia
Crabtree Publishing
3 Charles Street
Coburg North
VIC 3058

Contents

Protecting our Earth

Earth's surface is always changing. Some changes are good. Floods bring new soil to the land along rivers. The minerals in the soil help improve farmland. Volcanoes can also create new farmland full of minerals. Volcanoes in the ocean can create new islands.

These tomato plants are growing in rich volcanic soil in Spain.

Danger by land and sea

Some changes to Earth's surface are not good. Earthquakes can destroy land and buildings. **Tsunamis** wash away homes and damage coastlines. Water and wind can strip the soil from farmland. Scientists are working to better understand these forces. They want to find ways to slow these forces or prevent them from happening.

If scientists better understand Earth's forces, they can help people prepare for dangerous changes.

Quick changes

Changes to Earth's surface can happen quickly or slowly. Volcanoes, earthquakes, and floods are some ways the surface changes quickly. Volcanoes are openings in Earth's surface. When a volcano **erupts**, hot, melted rock from deep underground is pushed out of the opening. **Lava** flowing out from a volcano covers everything in its path. The lava then cools into new rock.

Lava glows red hot as it flows.

On the move

Earthquakes cause Earth's surface to shake suddenly. This can create cracks in the ground and cause buildings to fall. Floods can move a lot of soil and rocks in a short time. Floodwater is strong enough to move huge rocks. The running water can carve out deep **channels** in the soil.

During the 2015 earthquake in Nepal, the ground around the city of Kathmandu rose by 3 feet (1 meter)!

What do you think?

Why are earthquakes, floods, and volcanoes dangerous for people?

Slow changes

Erosion happens when material moves from one place to another. It can happen quickly during floods. It can also happen very slowly. Wind can erode soil from farmland. Over time, rock is all that is left. Streams and rivers also remove soil. Water slowly erodes the land along the sides of rivers. This can create a **canyon**.

Glaciers are rivers of ice. They move slowly down a mountain and erode the land in their path.

Wearing away

Wind can blow tiny bits of rock at **landforms**. This can cause small pieces of the landforms to break off. Landforms can wear away over time. This wearing down is called weathering. Once a landform has been weathered, erosion can move it.

Weathering can change the size and shape of landforms over time.

Doing harm

Erosion and weathering are happening all the time. Sometimes they can be harmful to the land and the people living on it. Erosion can happen quickly during a heavy rain. Rocks on hillsides can come loose and soil can turn to mud. The mud and rocks can slide down the hill in a landslide.

A large part of a hill can be lost in a landslide.

Losing ground

Erosion can be harmful to farmland. Rich soil can be blown away by wind. This means less land for farmers to grow food. The blowing soil can fall into rivers, streams, and ponds. This can cause the water to become **polluted**. The soil in the water blocks sunlight from reaching the plants below. Plants need sunlight to live.

What do you think?

Why is water pollution harmful for plants living in lakes and streams?

A plastic cover can help stop soil erosion.

Human hands

Humans can also cause harmful changes to Earth's surface. The roots of trees and plants help hold soil in place. Clearing land for farming means the soil will be loose. When soil is loose, there is more chance of erosion from wind or water.

Building dams changes the way a river moves. This can affect the fish living in it.

Changing landscape

When people put in new roads, the land changes. It is flattened for safer driving. Hills are removed and valleys are filled in with soil. **Mining** leaves large holes in the ground. The land above mines can fall in.

New roads change the land. There are fewer trees and plants to help stop erosion from wind and water.

Problem solvers

Information from scientists lets us know the best ways to stop erosion.

Scientists are working hard to understand erosion. They meet to share ideas. This is called brainstorming. Brainstorming helps to plan **experiments** and create new tools. Scientists have learned new ways of measuring soil loss.

Using models

Scientists sometimes build models to help them understand a problem. A model is a small copy of something larger. A model of a shoreline is very useful. Scientists can use the model to study how waves erode the coast. They can also test new ways to protect beaches from eroding.

Scientists might use models to track shifting sandbars, such as these in Humboldt Bay, California. This will help keep waterways safe for boats.

sandbars

Making it better

There are many ways people can help slow erosion. Wind can easily blow away loose soil. One way to protect soil is to cover it. Plants, such as grass, shrubs, and trees, cover soil. The roots of plants help hold the soil in place.

Farmers can also plant tall trees around their fields to block some of the wind from hitting their **crops***. These are called windbreaks.*

Plant protection

Plants can help stop landslides from happening, too. People can plant trees and shrubs on hills. During heavy rains, the roots help hold the soil in place. Heavy rains can also cause rivers to rise and flood nearby land. Levees help hold back water and stop the land from eroding. A levee is a wall or grassy hill on the side of a river.

Grass planted on earth levees keep them from washing away.

Small scale

People and communities can play a big part in slowing and stopping erosion. Grass in sports fields often gets ripped up from a lot of use. This leaves the soil uncovered and at risk for erosion. Planting new grass will help protect the soil for the next season.

Trees help stop erosion with their roots, and also with their leaves. Leaves help stop heavy rain from washing away the soil below them.

Channeling rainwater

Ditches channel rainwater away from bare fields and dirt roads. Rainwater can cause ditches to erode. Planting grass in the ditches can help slow down erosion.

What do you think?

How can planting trees along a river help with erosion?

Planting a flower or vegetable garden in bare ground is another way to stop soil erosion.

Washed away activity

This activity shows erosion in action. You will be able to see how easily bare ground erodes. You can also see how other materials can slow erosion.

You will need:

Shallow box or pan

A jug or cup of water

Soil

Books or blocks to prop up pan about 1 inch (2.5 cm)

Materials such as sticks, rocks, netting, leaves

Steps

1. Place soil in the shallow pan. Prop up one end of the pan on books or blocks.
2. Slowly pour the water on the soil at the higher end. Watch what happens to the soil.
3. Put the pan back on level ground and make the soil level again.
4. Add sticks and leaves to the soil.
5. Pour the water again. Watch what happens.
6. Set a line of rocks across the middle of the pan.
7. Pour the water again. Watch what happens.
8. Place the netting into the soil to act like plant roots.
9. Pour the water again. Watch what happens.

Asking questions

- What happened to the soil when you first poured the water onto it?
- What changed when the sticks, leaves, and rocks were added?
- What difference did the netting make?

Your help

Erosion is a big problem. We can all do things to help slow it down. Take a walk through your neighborhood with a family member or friend. Look for ways you can help slow erosion in your community.

Brainstorm with others to find ways you can help protect Earth's surface.

Learning more

Books

Erosion: Changing Earth's Surface by Robin Koontz,
Picture Window Books, 2007.

Examining Erosion by Joelle Riley, Lerner Publishing Group, 2013.

Soil Erosion and How to Prevent It by Natalie Hyde,
Crabtree Publishing, 2010.

Websites

Tips on how kids can help prevent soil erosion and a fun activity:
www.ecoallstarkids.com/Soil.aspx

Geography4Kids talks about erosion, with a great video showing coastal
erosion: **www.geography4kids.com/files/land_erosion.html**

Learn some interesting facts about erosion from Ducksters:
www.ducksters.com/science/earth_science/erosion.php

Words to know

canyon (KAN-yuh n) noun A narrow, deep valley with steep sides

channels (CHAN-lz) noun Grooves in the ground made by flowing water

crops (kropz) noun Plants grown by farmers

ditches (dich-es) noun Narrow trenches dug in the ground

erupts (ih-RUHPTS) verb Explodes with lava and ash

experiments (ik-SPER-uh-muh nts) noun Tests to see if an idea is true

landforms (LAND-fawrmz) noun Features on Earth's surface

lava (LAV-uh) noun Melted rock that flows out of a volcano

mining (MAHY-nin) noun Digging in the ground for ores and minerals

polluted (puh-LOO-tid) adjective Full of harmful materials

tsunamis (tsoo-NAH-meez) noun Huge waves caused by an earthquake underwater

A noun is a person, place, or thing. A verb is an action word that tells you what someone or something does. An adjective is a word that tells you what something is like.

Index

24